THE HOLY SPIRIT
IS A GENIUS

IF YOU LISTEN TO HIM,

● ●

HE WILL MAKE YOU LOOK SMART

● ●

THE HOLY SPIRIT
IS A GENIUS
IF YOU LISTEN TO HIM,
•••••••••••••••••••••••••••••••••
HE WILL MAKE YOU LOOK SMART
•••••••••••••••••••••••••••••••

MARK HANKINS

Unless otherwise indicated, all scriptural quotations are from the King James Version of the Bible.

The Holy Spirit is a Genius
ISBN #978-1-889981-64-2

First Edition 2019

Published By
MHM Publications
P.O. Box 12863
Alexandria, LA 71315
www.markhankins.org

Printed in the United States of America.

TABLE OF CONTENTS

*When the Holy Spirit
is working on our case
we have a tremendous
advantage. He has
a reputation for
winning cases.*

1

THE HOLY SPIRIT -
THE GENIUS

The Holy Ghost is not just smart; He is a genius. When you listen, cooperate with, and respond to Him, He will make you look smart.

The Holy Ghost is a genius. If you will listen to Him, He will make you look smart.

B. B. Hankins

Since He is a genius, He knows everything. He knows the mind of God and everything that Jesus has purchased for us. It is great to have a genius living in you. The Holy Ghost is also a gentleman and will not interrupt you. Until you stop and recognize Him, He will allow you to keep doing what you are doing. You must stop and say, "Alright, what would the Genius like to say?"

The Holy Spirit is the head of God's revelation department. God's kingdom system of revelation knowledge has never been hacked. You can steal information, but you can't steal revelation. The blood and the Holy Spirit give us access to the wisdom of God. The blood and the Holy Spirit are inseparable. Where the blood of Jesus is honored, the Holy Spirit will work. What the blood of Jesus has done in Heaven, the Holy Spirit is doing in our hearts. Where the blood of Jesus flows, the Holy Spirit goes. Smith Wigglesworth said, "The Holy Spirit never brings condemnation but always reveals the blood of Christ." (Hebrews 10:14-22)

I heard Kenneth E. Hagin (Dad Hagin) say the Lord told him, "If we would be led by the Holy Spirit He would make us rich." He said the word "rich" means to have an abundant supply. If we are led by the Holy Spirit, He will bring us into the blessing of the Lord and we will be a blessing to others. The Holy Spirit will help you in every area of your life. He will help you know who to marry, where to work, what kind of car to buy, when to buy a house, and what to do with your money. The Holy Ghost is a genius. He knows everything.

> *So shall they fear the name of the LORD from the west, and his glory from the rising of the sun. When the enemy shall come in like a flood, the Spirit of the LORD shall lift up a standard against him.*
>
> *Isaiah 59:19*

When the enemy has a scheme or strategy to come against you or your family, the Holy Spirit will warn you. He's a genius. He knows what the devil has planned. The Holy Spirit also knows what God has planned for you. He is concerned with every area of your life. If you will listen to Him, He will make you successful.

THE MIND OF A GENIUS

The death, burial, resurrection of Christ, and the Word of God are essential to faith. However, if that was all you needed, God would not have sent the Holy Spirit. *The Holy Spirit takes what Jesus has done for us and translates it into personal victory.* In John 14, 15, and 16, Jesus teaches a lot about the Holy Spirit. Whole chapters of Paul's epistles are devoted to teaching on the work of the Holy Spirit. The Holy Spirit transmits the mind of Christ to us, but we must learn to recognize, respond and yield to Him. We can think like God thinks when we are filled with the Holy Spirit. *If you want to study the mind of a genius, be filled with the Holy Spirit.* The Holy Spirit takes all your receiving from God into a whole new dimension (1 Corinthians 2:12-14). He gives uncommon intelligence, insight, and understanding.

> *The world needs to be taught to receive Jesus but the church needs to be taught to receive the Holy Spirit.*
> *Rev. Kenneth E. Hagin*

The greatest need for any person is Jesus because salvation comes from knowing Him. However, after a person gets saved, they need to be filled with the Holy Spirit. We know that the Holy Spirit is extremely powerful, but He is also a gentleman. He comes to do His work where He is acknowledged, recognized and invited. The moment anyone opens the door to the Holy Spirit, He magnifies Jesus.

Smith Wigglesworth said that with the power of the Holy Ghost, he was a thousand times bigger on the inside than on the outside! He is the greater one.

Paul's prayer in Eph. 3:14-21 is to be strengthened with mighty power according to the riches of God's glory in the inner man. The Holy Spirit is not far from the believer—He is on the inside! He supplies strength to the things in your character that may be weak. He brings a change of voice and vision to the person who has a strong inner man.

We must recognize Him living within. T.L. Osborn said, ***"The Christian can say what no other religion can say: 'My God lives in me!'"*** Without the Holy Spirit, Jesus is only a historical figure, but with Him, Jesus is *IN* you! The Holy Spirit's assignment is to take all that Jesus has done *for* us and make it a reality *in* us.

THE COMFORTER

The word "Comforter" does not only mean consolation or sympathy in sorrow or distress. We are not talking about a big pillow or blanket. No, it means much more. The Greek word is "Parakletos" and William Barclay describes the Holy Spirit's work in this way:

The function of the Holy Spirit is to fill a man with the spirit of power and courage which would make

11

him triumphantly cope with life. The narrowing of the word "comforter" has resulted in the undue narrowing of the work of the Holy Spirit.

With the Holy Spirit's help, you have a Comforter, someone to stand by you, and a Counselor, one who befriends you. Jesus didn't leave us alone or as orphans, but when He sent the Holy Spirit (the Helper) He gave us a great advantage in life, in prayer and in direction.

In John 16:7 in the Amplified Bible, Jesus called the Holy Spirit the ***Parakletos***, which includes Counselor, Helper, Advocate, Intercessor, Strengthener and Standby. The Holy Spirit comes to make you strong and to help you to stand. He will not only help you stand, but win your case.

WIN THE CASE

P.C. Nelson wrote the book of fundamental Bible doctrines for the Assemblies of God. He was a Greek and Hebrew scholar, fluent in 32 different languages. He explains the Holy Spirit, our Advocate, has excellence in three areas: ***1) Exceptional knowledge, 2) Expertise in protocol and procedure, 3) Persuasive speaking ability.*** When the Holy

Spirit is working on our case, we have a tremendous advantage. He has a reputation for winning cases.

THE PARAKLETOS:
THE ADVOCATE OR LEGAL DEFENSE

William Barclay in his study of *New Testament Words* has these enlightening comments about two Greek words describing who the Holy Spirit is and what His work is in the life of a believer.

The ***Parakletos*** is one who does these things:

- *He is called in to render service.*
- *He is called in to help in a situation with which a man by himself cannot cope.*
- *He will keep a man on his feet when left to himself would collapse. The Holy Spirit enables him to pass the breaking point and not break.*
- *He is the friend of the accused person. He is called in to support his character, in order to enlist the sympathy of the judge in his favor.*
- *He is the counsel of the defense, someone who will present someones case to another person in a most favorable light.*

13

THE PARAKALEIN: THE ONE WHO CHEERS THE FAINT HEARTED

The classic Greek use of the verb, **Parakalein** is quite interesting. William Barclay describes this word like this:

Military leaders or generals who exhort troops who are going into battle, rallying and cheering them to fight and to accept the risk of battle. It is like the speech the general gives to leaders and soldiers, cheering them on before battle. He puts courage into the faint-hearted; He makes a very ordinary person cope gallantly with a very perilous and dangerous situation.

It is a luxury to be filled with the Spirit, and at the same time it is a divine command.

Smith Wigglesworth

2

THE DIVINE COMMAND:

BE FILLED WITH THE HOLY SPIRIT

The Holy Spirit has never lost a case if He can get His client to listen to Him. The Holy Spirit has a reputation for working with some real losers and making them champions.

I like what Smith Wigglesworth said: "God has put us in a place where He expects us to have His latest revelation, the revelation of that marvelous fact of ***Christ in [us]*** (Col. 1:27) and what this really means. We can understand Christ fully only as we are filled and overflowing with the Spirit of God. Our only safeguard from dropping back into our natural minds, from which we can never get anything, is to be filled and filled again with the Spirit of God, and to be taken on to new visions and revelations." Wigglesworth also said, ***"It is a luxury to be filled with the Spirit, and at the same time it is a divine command."***

I used to play football in my backyard with the neighborhood boys. It was usually the guys my age against my older brother and his friends. What we lacked in size we made up for in great desire and determination to show how tough we were. I will never forget the day I was running a long route and turned around to catch a pass. After I caught the ball, I turned to run and at that moment I came in direct contact with the window air conditioner. It knocked me down, shook me up and I lost my wind, but I remember looking up at the boys' faces looking down at me and saying these words, "I still have the ball!"

Sometimes circumstances, people, or the enemy himself may knock you down. You may have people watching to see if you're giving up. Or maybe you wonder if you have what it takes to win in your situation. Remember, the Paraklete, the Helper, the Greater One is in you to cheer, defend and strengthen you. The comfort He brings will revive you and bring increase as you cooperate with Him.

When Paul wrote Romans 8:26 he may have had this comfort and strength in mind.

Likewise the Spirit also helpeth our infirmities: for we know not what we should pray for as we ought: but the Spirit itself maketh intercession for us with groanings which cannot be uttered.

Romans 8:26

The Holy Spirit takes hold together with us, against our weakness, to pray. His life, His resurrection power, and great strength through us to bring forth the will of God.

David encouraged himself in the Lord. The Lord stood by Paul in a storm to tell him to be of good cheer or comfort. Like these men, we are commanded and able to be strong in the Lord and in the power of His might.

FILLED WITH ALL OF GOD

When you yield to the Holy Spirit, many things take place. One thing is that you become filled and flooded with God Himself. All of you is filled with all of God. Paul's prayer is that the church will be *"wholly filled and flooded with God Himself,"* Ephesians 3:19 (AMP).

The Holy Spirit comes to strengthen your inner man, and transform your vision, your voice, and bring revelation knowledge. One way to be strengthened is to build yourself up on your most holy faith, praying in the Spirit (Jude 20). Then you may be able to grasp all the dimensions of the love of God, and be filled and flooded with God Himself. When you are filled with God, you know what He has done in Christ. That's when you can experience the exceeding greatness of His resurrection power released to every believer.

SEISMIC RETROFIT

The Holy Ghost never comes on you or works in you just to make you look good. He is actually strategically strengthening you in areas of your life so you can face any situation. When the storm is over and the dust clears, you will still be standing.

Years ago, I was driving through San Diego and noticed that some of the buildings had cables running from each of their corners to the ground. I had never seen that on a building before, so I wanted to know what it was. I found out that it was called seismic retrofit. The cables strategically strengthen these buildings so that when an earthquake hits, they will not collapse. These buildings are strengthened from corner to corner, inside and outside, so after the shaking of an earthquake, they will still stand.

I believe the Holy Ghost can give you some seismic retrofit. You may not have certain strengths in your life, but the Holy Ghost will add things to you. He will strengthen you in your inner man. When the devil shakes you, you can say, "I'm still standing." Thank God for the Holy Spirit who is our Strengthener.

Life wasn't meant to go through sober! Be filled with the Holy Spirit.

3

DRINK BETTER -
THINK BETTER

And be not drunk with wine, wherein is excess; but be filled with the Spirit; speaking to yourselves in psalms and hymns and spiritual songs, singing and making melody in your heart to the Lord.

Ephesians 5:18,19

Don't get drunk on wine...TANK UP ON THE SPIRIT. (Jordan)

Drink the Spirit of God, huge draughts of Him. (MSG)

The most important thing, the one thing that counts, is to see that we are filled with the Holy Spirit, filled to overflowing. Anything less than this is displeasing to God. We are commanded by God to be filled with the Spirit, and in the measure you fail of this, you are that far short of the plan of God. Our only safeguard from dropping back into our natural minds, from which we can never get anything, is to be filled and yet filled again with the Spirit of God, and to be taken on to visions and revelations.

Smith Wigglesworth

In Acts 2, Peter compares being filled with the Holy Spirit to drinking wine. We know on the day of Pentecost the people in the upper room were filled with the Holy Spirit and accused of being drunk. They were so filled with the Holy Spirit they appeared intoxicated. They had been drinking from the Holy Spirit until they were filled and under the influence. Throughout the book of Acts, the disciples were filled (continuously) with the Holy Spirit and joy (Acts 13:52). **The Holy Spirit and joy are always connected.** Even the anointing of the Holy Spirit is called the oil of joy (Hebrews 1:9).

The anointing of the Holy Spirit will make you lose your mind and get the mind of Christ. How great

it is to stop thinking and start drinking. Stop trying
to figure out God with your intellect, and receive the
Holy Spirit. He will take the things of Christ and show
them to you. You enter the realm of revelation when
you are filled with the Spirit. When you drink better
you will think better.

UNDER THE INFLUENCE

No one ever got drunk on wine by just *thinking*.
No! You get drunk by drinking. If someone got arrested
for driving under the influence, they could tell the
police officer that they went to a bar but they were only
sitting in there thinking. However, the officer would
know that they didn't get drunk by thinking. They
had to be drinking to get drunk. The same is true
with the Holy Spirit. *You must have a drinking
relationship with the Spirit of God.*

OPEN YOUR MOUTH WIDE

One thing I know about drinking is that you
cannot drink with your mouth shut. Job 29:23 says,
"...and they opened their mouth wide as for the latter
rain." The latter rain is a type of the outpouring of
the Holy Spirit. Again in Psalms 81:10, "...open thy
mouth wide and I will fill it." As we open our mouth
and begin to drink, God fills our mouth with good

things. He fills our mouth and our hearts with His presence. He fills our mouth with laughter. He fills us with His strength. Notice the connection between drinking and speaking or praising. As we open our mouth and lift our voice, the drinking has begun. The Holy Spirit overflows like mighty rivers flowing from our innermost being.

THIRSTY...COME AND DRINK

In John 7:37-39, Jesus said, "If any man thirst, let him come unto me and drink. He that believeth on me, as the scripture hath said, out of his belly shall flow rivers of living water. But this spake he of the Holy Spirit...." Notice Jesus said to come and drink. He was telling us something supernatural happens in us when we fellowship with Him and the Holy Spirit. Rivers of living (Zoe-God's life) waters flow freely. This is not natural water, but is water from Heaven and something is in this water. Everything that is in God is in this water—wisdom, healing, joy, peace, satisfaction, and love. We must drink daily from His presence.

The Holy Spirit could not be given until the blood of Jesus was shed at the cross and applied in Heaven by Jesus after He was raised from the dead. The power of the blood of Jesus and the Holy Spirit work together to bring God's grace and mercy in overflowing measure into our hearts.

And he showed me a pure river of water of life, clear as crystal, proceeding out of the throne of God and of the lamb. And the Spirit and the bride say, Come. And let him that heareth say, Come. And let him that is athirst come. And whosoever will, let him take the water of life freely.

Revelation 22:1, 17

God is still looking for drinkers. Who will come and drink? Jesus cries out for those who are thirsty to drink. He told the woman at the well if you drink from this water you will never thirst again (John 4:13-14). It will satisfy your longing soul. If you drink this water it will spring up within you. This is living water. Everything lives where this water flows. Sometimes we need drinking lessons or drinking friends to receive all that God has for us. Open your mouth wide and God will fill it.

Receiving the Holy Spirit and speaking in tongues will take all your receiving to a whole new dimension.

4

THE CODE TALKERS

During World War II, there was tremendous fighting in the Pacific region against the Japanese who were taking over nation after nation. U.S. troops suffered many casualties because their radio messages were being intercepted and deciphered by the enemy. Military commanders had always searched for a perfect code that couldn't be broken, and someone found that Navajo soldiers spoke a "hidden language" used only in their family. At that time, this language had no alphabet or symbols and had never been written down. So Navajo men were trained and sent to the Pacific to use their language as the secret code that saved lives and won battles.

One of the Japanese said, "What is that language? It sounds like they're talking under water." To them it didn't sound like much, but it was the "Navajo Code Talkers" or "Windtalkers" speaking an intelligent language. The code talkers were very valuable and they took part in every assault the U.S. Marines conducted in the Pacific from 1942 to 1945. They began with 29 men in 1942 and grew to over 400 men serving in 1945. Since there are no military terms in the Navajo language, when developing the code, the Navajo Code Talkers got creative with Navajo words. For example, a bomber plane was "Jay-sho," which means buzzard. None of the Navajo Code Talkers could speak about the highly classified program until after the war. The code was never broken by the Japanese.

Because the code talkers were so valuable, each one was protected by a Marine. When U.S. soldiers were pinned down, the Navajo Code Talkers could send a message in two minutes instead of what used to take hours. Their messages gave troop locations and brought in air support and the big guns. They risked their lives to get to a radio to deliver their messages to the Command post. The Navajo code was vital to the victory in Saipan and every major battle in the Pacific.

SPEAKING IN TONGUES, THE SPIRIT CODE

In the kingdom of God, we are in a battle with the powers of darkness – a battle more intense and crucial than those fought in the Pacific area. Lives and nations are being lost and we must have the help of the Holy Spirit to bring the saving message of Jesus. Jesus would not have sent the Holy Spirit if we didn't need His help to do this important work of taking the Gospel to the World.

On the day of Pentecost, a sound like a mighty wind was heard and the Holy Spirit filled believers. God gave the church a supernatural "code language" the devil could not break. "And they were all filled with the Holy Ghost, and began to speak with other tongues, as the Spirit gave them utterance" (Acts 2:4). *With that prayer language, Spirit-filled believers worship God, but they can also declare holy information, activate Heaven's troops and send reinforcements. Just as each Navajo Code Talkers was protected by a Marine, believers have angels assigned to protect them.*

In the same way the Navajo code communicated secrets and plans, speaking in tongues is a spiritual language given by God to allow believers to communicate with Him. Praying in the Spirit is the exchange of divine secrets with God. 1 Corinthians 14:2 says, ***"For he that speaketh in an unknown tongue speaketh not unto men, but unto God: for no man understandeth him; howbeit in the spirit he speaketh mysteries."*** In verse 18 Paul says, "I thank my God I speak with tongues more than you all." Paul valued praying in tongues, and he wished all the Corinthians spoke with tongues (1 Corinthians 14:5)!

GOD'S HEAD BY-PASS OPERATION

I call speaking with tongues "God's head by-pass operation." Why would God want to by-pass your head? You should know the answer to that! One reason is that you have blockages there, and your thinking needs to change.

Religion and the devil will fight you about speaking in tongues. Dad Hagin told how he, as a young minister, determined to pray in the Spirit for one hour. His mind and the devil tried to discourage him, telling him he was wasting his time. Dad Hagin said, "Devil, since you said that, I'm going to pray in tongues for another hour." This struggle kept up, hour after hour, with thoughts like, "You've wasted four hours. You could have been mowing the lawn, visiting the sick or preparing your sermon." Imagine the devil hating speaking in tongues so much that he suggests you quit and go study for your message! Instead of quitting, he told the devil, "Just because you said that, I'm going to pray another hour." In the fifth hour Dad Hagin said he hit what he called "a gusher!" He said once he hit that gusher it never took him five hours again to pray with such freedom.

You see, when you pray in tongues, the devil can't get in on it, so he wants to stop you. You're talking to God, speaking divine secrets, and praying out God's perfect will (Romans 8:26-28). ***The way you yield to the Holy Spirit is the same way you yield to all the will of God.***

SPIRITUAL STRENGTH

Spiritual strength is one of the many benefits to speaking in tongues. Jude 20 says we build up ourselves on our most holy faith praying in the Spirit. It takes faith to speak in tongues, so when you speak with tongues, your faith is strengthened. Your tongue is the most difficult member of your body to control, so if you yield it to the Holy Spirit, you will gain victory in other areas. Many have even testified they received their healing when they were filled with the Holy Spirit, speaking in tongues.

Speaking in tongues will help you yield to the fruit of the Spirit in your spirit instead of yielding to physical passions. Galatians 5:22 (AMP) describes the work of the Holy Spirit in the life of a believer like this: *"But the fruit of the [Holy] Spirit [the work which His presence within accomplishes]...."* The fruit His presence brings is love, joy, peace, long-suffering, gentleness, goodness, faith, meekness, and temperance or self-control.

There was a certain evangelist staying at the home of the pastor of the church where he was speaking. One afternoon he came out of the bedroom and overheard the pastor's daughter arguing with her mother. The girl had lost her temper. When the girl looked up and saw the minister, she was very ashamed of her actions. After she apologized, the minister encouraged the girl to pray in tongues. He said that if she would do so, the Holy Spirit would help her control her temper. Years later, that same girl, now grown up, happened to see the minister. She thanked him for the advice he had given her. Because she practiced praying in tongues, she grew stronger spiritually and never lost her temper like that again.

Receiving the Holy Spirit and speaking in tongues will take all your receiving to a whole new dimension. Speaking in tongues will take your prayer life to another level, strengthen your spirit, and give you an advantage over Satan's strategies. It will even open up financial resources, give you access to holy information the enemy can't understand, and you will win in areas where you were previously defeated. When you're filled with the Holy Spirit, He thinks through your mind, changes your personality and magnifies Jesus. The code of the Spirit helps you activate and fulfill the plan and purpose of God.

We must not forget that praying in tongues is not only the initial evidence of the Holy Spirit's indwelling; it is the continual experience for the rest of one's life. For what purpose? To assist in the worship of God. Speaking in tongues is a flowing stream that should never dry up, for it will enrich a person's life spiritually.

Howard Carter

The Holy Spirit has a reputation for working with some real losers and making them champions.

5

THE HOLY SPIRIT - OUR FIRST RESPONDER

In the book of Genesis 1 we see that in the beginning the earth was without form, and void and darkness was upon the face of the deep. Everything was out of order, dark, ugly and full of chaos. It was then that the Spirit of God moved on the face of the waters. The Spirit of God saw the earth in a mess and the Holy Spirit jumped in the middle of that mess. The Holy Spirit moved on the face of the deep and God said let there be light and creation began. Everything that was ugly became beautiful.

The Holy Spirit is not afraid of any kind of mess. He is like a first responder, coming just when you need

Him. He gets in the pit with you, in your weakness or struggle and takes you to victory. The Holy Spirit has a reputation for working with some real losers and making them champions.

> *Likewise the Spirit also helpeth our infirmities: for we know not what we should pray for as we ought: but the Spirit itself maketh intercession for us with groanings which cannot be uttered. And he that searcheth the hearts knoweth what is the mind of the Spirit, because he maketh intercession for the saints according to the will of God.*
>
> *Romans 8:26-27*

Rick Renner gives light on the full meaning of the word *infirmities* in the Greek. He says it describes *a crippling disease, a mental oppression, a recurring plague which is terminal and incurable.* So, you need help and the Holy Spirit wants to help! The Holy Spirit helps you overcome and win in a situation that seem incurable or hopelessly recurring. In the Greek, the word *helpeth* means "to take hold together with you against" your infirmity.

The Spirit helps by making intercession for you with "groanings which cannot be uttered."

An example of this is when a person has fallen into a pit and cannot get out without help. This is when the *Spirit of God gets into the pit with you, makes intercession, and lifts you out.* He shares your feelings. The Holy Spirit helps you pray beyond your natural language, with groanings that cannot be uttered (Romans 8:26). P.C. Nelson said the Greek means with groanings that can't be uttered in our articulate speech. This not only includes groanings, but also includes speaking in other tongues which is a supernatural language of the Holy Spirit to help us.

Knowing that the Holy Spirit is always ready to help us, we understand that *the only way a Christian can be defeated is if he is spiritually depleted.* Jude 20 says, "But ye, beloved, building up yourselves on your most holy faith, praying in the Holy Ghost." The New English Bible uses the words "fortify yourself." The Amplified Bible says, "make spiritual progress."

When we speak in tongues or pray in the Spirit, our spirit is connected to God and we are charged up. A great example of this is the cell phone. When your cell phone is properly charged, you are connected to unlimited apps, people, and information. When your spirit is charged up, you are empowered to keep your mind, emotions and feelings from dominating you.

Speaking in tongues releases resurrection power that will lift you out of any pit you have found yourself in. One translation of Romans 8:11 says, *"**God raised Jesus from the dead, and if God's Spirit is living in you, he will also give life to your bodies that die. God is the One who raised Christ from the dead, and he will give life through his Spirit that lives in you. He will bring to your whole being new strength and vitality.**"* .

HOW TO WIN IN LIFE'S DEEPEST STRUGGLES

And the very God of peace sanctify you wholly; and I pray God your whole spirit and soul and body be preserved blameless unto the coming of our Lord Jesus Christ.

1 Thessalonians 5:23

In 1 Thessalonians 5:23, Paul tells us the three-part nature of man: he is a spirit, he has a soul and lives in a body. This is like a transparency that can be laid over everything Paul teaches. Knowing this gives us understanding of how it is possible to experience victory in every area of life. Your spirit, or pneuma, is the real you, looking out of your eyes. Your soul, or psuche in the Greek, is your mind, will and emotions which operate through your brain. The Greek word for body is soma, and it is designed to carry and express your spirit, the real you. At times the body, mind, feelings and emotions will seem stronger than your spirit and try to bully you, but through the power of the Spirit you can overcome. Dad Hagin said, "Anyone who shuts their spirit away and refuses to develop it will become crippled in life and a victim of scheming people." As believers we can grow spiritually through meditating on the Word of God and praying in the Holy Spirit.

James Stalker explains our deepest struggle in *The Life of St. Paul:*

> *The nature of man, according to Paul, normally consists of three sections - body, soul, and spirit (to emphasize proper order, I refer to it as spirit, soul and body). In his original constitution these occupied definite relations of superiority and subordination to one another, the spirit being supreme, the body least important, and the soul occupying the middle position.*

But the fall disarranged this order, and all sin consists in the usurpation by the body or the soul in the place of the spirit. In fallen man these two inferior sections of human nature, which together form what Paul calls the "flesh," or that side of human nature that looks toward the world and time, have taken possession of the throne and completely rule the life, while the spirit, the side of man that looks toward God and eternity, has been dethroned and reduced to a condition of inefficiency and death. Christ restores the lost predominance of the spirit of man by taking possession of it by His own Spirit. His Spirit dwells in the human spirit, vivifying it and sustaining it in such growing strength that it becomes more and more the sovereign part of man's constitution. The man ceases to be carnal and becomes spiritual; he is led by the Spirit of God and becomes more and more harmonious with all that is holy and divine.

There is a barn on my property where I used to keep my horses. One day a worker brought me the news that I had termites. Of course, we had to get rid of them, so we called the exterminator. I didn't fall to pieces about them, I didn't blame somebody or even try to figure out how they got there. It wasn't *me* who had the termites - ***my barn did.*** Likewise, if you have sin, bad habits, attitudes, etc, you don't have the "termites," but the house - your body, soul, mind - may have them. You can get rid of them through the power of the Spirit.

Paul explains it this way. "For if ye live after the flesh, ye shall die: but if ye through the Spirit do mortify the deeds of the body, ye shall live" (Romans 8:13). Wade's translation says, "...***if by the help of spiritual influences, you deal a death blow to the activities that originate with the body, you will live.***"

TRUST IN THE GOD WHO LIVES IN YOU

Remember that you belong to God. Goodspeed's translation of Romans 3:13 says, "...he who raised Christ Jesus from the dead will also give your mortal bodies life through his Spirit that has taken possession of you." Greater is He who is *IN* you! Remember what James Stalker said: Christ restores the lost predominance of the spirit of man by taking possession of it by His own Spirit.

It is God who is working in you both to will and to do of His good pleasure (Philippians 2:13). You are joined to the Lord and you form a single spirit in union with Him. Pray in the spirit, worship in the spirit, rejoice in the spirit, serve God in the spirit, walk in the spirit, and be strengthened in your spirit. As you speak in tongues you will open the door to all of the supernatural. As you yield to the Spirit, He will take things that are out of order and bring them into order.

The same power that is in the actual events of the death, burial, and resurrection of Christ is in the message of the Gospel. The devil is just as afraid of the message as he is of the events.

6

ENRICHED FAITH

I was reading the book, _How Stuff Work_, learning how such things as washing machines and car engines work. I came across the chapter called "How Nuclear Energy Works." It caught my attention. I began to compare natural energy with supernatural power. Nuclear power plants provide 17% of the world's electricity, as well as powering nuclear submarines and aircraft carriers. When a single atom splits, an incredible amount of energy is released. Uranium is the heaviest and the best example of a naturally radioactive element. The most commonly used isotope in creating nuclear power is a material called U-235.

When an atom undergoes fission, an immense amount of energy is produced. This process occurs quickly — in about one picosecond, or one millionth of a second. For fission to be effective, the uranium sample must be enriched so it contains 2-3% U-235. In a nuclear bomb, you want uranium to undergo fission as quickly as possible, releasing all the energy in an instant and creating a gigantic explosion. A pound of highly enriched uranium can be used to power a nuclear submarine or nuclear aircraft carrier and is equal to about a million gallons of gasoline. When you consider the fact that a pound of uranium is smaller than a baseball and a million gallons of gasoline would fill a container as tall as a five story building, you get an idea of the amount of energy available in just a little bit of enriched U-235!

THE PRAYER THAT ENRICHES FAITH

Just as uranium can be enriched, so can your faith. The first thing we need is knowledge of **dunamis,** the God kind of power. What is this dunamis power? It is inherent power; power for performing miracles; moral power and excellence of soul; the power and influence which belong to riches and wealth; power and resources arising from numbers; power consisting in or resting upon armies, forces, hosts.

This power is in the blood of Christ and it cleanses us from the very root of sin. This power is the same power that raised Jesus from the dead. In Ephesians, Paul gives us a prayer we can pray. These are some of the words used to describe the great power that raised Jesus from the dead.

> *And what is the exceeding greatness of His power to usward who believe, according to the working of His mighty power which He wrought in Christ when he raised Him from the dead, and set Him at His own right hand in the Heavenly places.*
>
> *Ephesians 1:19,20*

...the limitless scope (Translator's)

...incredibly immense strength (Johnson)

...great beyond measure (Laubach)

...extraordinary power...it is the enormous overmastering supremacy (Cornish)

...incredible outburst of his might (Centenary)

...transcendently great (Wade)

...super abounding greatness (Wuest)

Just think about the resurrection power used to raise Christ from the dead. It was the same identical power that made you a new creation when you confessed Jesus as Lord. It is activated when you believe and speak the language of faith in God. Romans 12:3 tells us God has given to every man a measure of this faith substance. It is like nuclear power, but much greater. It has the energy to explode and stop the power of darkness and death, to bring light and life.

Just as there is an exact formula to produce U-235, there is an exact formula of faith as well. The mountain moving formula which activates this resurrection power is believing with the heart and speaking with your mouth. It only takes a mustard seed of faith to move a mountain. It is the identical faith that God has. Jesus commanded us to have this God-kind of faith in Mark 11:22.

This faith can be enriched by praying in the language of the Holy Spirit. One of the first times I experienced this to be true was when, as a young man, I was on a trip to Africa to preach. I spent a whole day praying in tongues and really had no great feeling of power at the time. However, that night in the service, the power of God was present and many people were healed and set free. "But ye, beloved, building up yourselves on your most holy faith, praying in the Holy Ghost," Jude 20. "But you shall receive power after that the Holy Ghost is come upon you...," Acts 1:8. "Wait on the Lord, receive the power so you can run and not grow weary, walk and not faint" Isaiah 40:31.

PREACH THE GOSPEL:
RELEASE THE POWER

There is power to heal the sick and change lives in the Gospel. Jesus came, preached the Gospel, cast out devils, healed the sick and raised the dead. He commanded His followers to do the same. After the day of Pentecost, Christians went everywhere preaching that Jesus died, was buried, and raised up by the power of God on the third day. Everywhere they went, there were confirming signs of the power of God following the preaching of the Good News.

In Acts 14, when Paul preached in Lystra, a crippled man heard the Gospel and it gave him faith to be healed. Paul shouted at him, "Stand up on your feet!" And he leaped up and walked. Explosive energy called resurrection power was released as he believed the Gospel. ***The same power that is in the actual events of the death, burial, and resurrection of Christ is in the message of the Gospel. The devil is just as afraid of the message as he is of the events.***

That power has not changed and is available for believers to walk in today. The Holy Spirit is still confirming the Good News with signs and wonders. We can all preach the Gospel and release the dunamis power of God to this generation!

On the day of Pentecost, the 120 people in the Upper Room were baptized into this power which gave them the ability to do the same works Jesus did with the same boldness in prayer and preaching as Jesus had. These 120 people were immersed into the identical power that raised Jesus from death. They all began to speak in languages they had not learned, telling of God's goodness. Peter was so transformed by the power of the Holy Spirit that he preached mightily, and three thousand people were saved! The results of this baptism of ***dunamis*** power shook the world.

THE GOSPEL IS THE POWER OF GOD

For I am not ashamed of the gospel of Christ: for it is the power of God unto

salvation, to everyone that believeth; to the Jew first, and also to the Greek. For therein is the righteousness of God revealed from faith to faith: as it is written, The just shall live by faith.
Romans 1:16, 17

The power of God is revealed in the Gospel — a spoken message, which releases great joy. It makes you glad. It is the language of redemption. It comes from the Greek word, *evangelion*. This word, together with its rendering of "good tidings and glad tidings," occurs 108 times in the New Testament, none of which imply anything less than "finished redemption" in Christ. The classic Greek meaning is "Good news from the battlefield or a battlefield victory."

Paul defined the word **GOSPEL** as being the message of the death, the burial, and the resurrection of Christ. Much emphasis is given to the declaration and explanation of it, as the Gospel contains the power of God. When you preach it, the Holy Ghost will help you. Angels respond because they desire to look into it (1 Peter 1:12). This good news is not man-made, but was announced by angels to the shepherds. The shepherds responded by rejoicing with exceeding great joy.

Moreover, brethren, I declare unto you the gospel which I preached unto you... for I delivered unto you first of all that which I also received, how that Christ died for our sins according to the scriptures; and that he was buried, and that he rose again the third day according to the scriptures.
1 Corinthians 15:1,3,4

Here we see the Gospel is the telling of the message of the death, burial, and resurrection of Jesus. *The significance of the resurrection of Christ is determined by the nature of His death.* When we understand what happened on the cross, that Jesus took our curse, sin, and death, then we understand that His resurrection is our resurrection, our life, our blessing and our victory. *Everything God did in Christ, in His death, burial, and resurrection was for us and is set to the credit of our account.*

[For my determined purpose is] that I may know Him [that I may progressively become more deeply and intimately acquainted with Him, perceiving and recognizing the wonders of His person more strongly

and more clearly], and that I may in the same way come to know the power outflowing from His resurrection [which it exerts over believers], and that I may so share His sufferings as to be continually transformed [in spirit into His likeness even] to His death.

Philippians 3:10, AMP

The more Paul walked with the Lord, suffered persecution, preached in the regions beyond, and was caught up in the Spirit, the more he desired to know Christ. After pouring out his life for the Church, going on his three missionary journeys and witnessing signs and wonders, the most significant experience of Paul's life was the revelation of the death, burial, and resurrection of Jesus Christ, and the revelation of his union with Christ. The deepest cry of his heart was to know Him, not to keep the Law, but to possess Christ's righteousness by faith.

The Holy Spirit takes everything Jesus has done for you and makes it real to you.

7

UNCOMMON STRENGTH

There is a funny story about a country boy who cut trees for a living. You might call him a "redneck." He heard of a new piece of equipment that was supposed to make work a lot easier and faster called a chainsaw. He bought one from the store because the man said he could cut up to 30 trees a day with this new chainsaw. After using it for a few days, he took it back to the store and complained that he was only able to cut 2 or 3 trees a day. The store manager took the chainsaw from him and pulled the starter rope. With a loud noise, the chainsaw started. The country boy jumped back, startled by the noise, and said, "What is that?" Being as ignorant as he was, he had never cranked the engine!

Today, many struggle in the work of the Lord because they have never been filled with the Holy Spirit. He is the power that enables us in every area of life. We must give the Holy Spirit His proper place everyday. My Dad always said, "The Holy Spirit is a genius. If you will listen to Him, He will make you look smart." So, if you ignore the Holy Spirit, you will not look very smart. Jesus said that you shall receive power after the Holy Spirit is come upon you. We thank God for the Holy Spirit. He is the Greater One who lives in us.

THE COMFORTER HAS COME

Before Jesus went to the cross and ascended to Heaven, He spent much time teaching on the Holy Ghost.

And I will pray the Father, and he shall give you another Comforter, that he may abide with you forever; even the Spirit of truth; whom the world cannot receive, because it seeth him not, neither knoweth him: but you know him; for he dwelleth with you, and shall be in you.

John 14:16, 17

Nevertheless I tell you the truth; it is expedient for you that I go away: for if I go not away, the Comforter will not come unto you; but if I depart, I will send him unto you.

John 16:7

The Holy Spirit will guide you into all truth and show you things to come. He will show, declare, and transmit the things of God the Father and the Lord Jesus Christ to you. Jesus said the Holy Spirit will move in you and dwell in you. He will bring you into close fellowship with the Father and the Lord Jesus. *The Holy Spirit takes everything Jesus has done for you and makes it real to you.* He is the power and presence of the risen and triumphant Christ *in you*.

UNCOMMON STRENGTH

The prayer of the Apostle Paul in Ephesians 3:14-21 describes the kind of strength that the Holy Spirit supplies in the inner man of every believer. He strengthens us with mighty power, fills us with the fullness of God, and opens the supernatural for exceeding abundant blessing.

For this cause I bow my knees unto the Father of our Lord Jesus Christ, of whom the whole family in heaven and earth is named, that He would grant you, according to the riches of his glory, to be strengthened with might by His Spirit in the inner man; that Christ may dwell in your hearts by faith; that ye, being rooted and grounded in love, may be able to comprehend with all the saints what is the breadth and length and depth and height; and to know the love of Christ which passes knowledge; that you may be filled with all the fulness of God. Now unto Him who is able to do exceedingly abundantly above all that we ask or think, according to the power that works in us, be glory in the church by Christ Jesus throughout all generations, forever and ever. Amen.

Ephesians 3:14-21

For believers, there are four ways to strengthen or charge our spirits. One way we do this is by ***praying in the Spirit***. Jude 20 says to build yourself up on your most holy faith, praying in the Holy Ghost. 1

Corinthians 14:2 says that when we pray in the Spirit, we are edified, built up, or charged. Another way we strengthen our spirits is by ***feeding on the Word.*** Matthew 4:4 says that man shall not live by bread alone, but by every word of God. A proper diet of the Word of God is key to strong faith. We also charge our spirits when we maintain ***supernatural relationships.*** God has designed the body of Christ with "joints" and "ligaments" knit together for the supply of nourishment (Colossians 2:19). Fellowship with Christ and one another is essential for this supply. "Let's see how inventive we can be in encouraging love and helping out, not avoiding worshiping together as some do but spurring each other on, especially as we see the big Day approaching," Hebrews 10:24,25 (MSG). Another way we stay strengthened in our spirits is by ***speaking the Word and praising God.*** "Out of the mouths of babes and infants, you have established strength," (Psalm 8:2). God has ordained strength to come out of our mouths, to stop the enemy.

IT IS NOT WASTED TIME

They that wait upon the Lord shall renew their strength.

Isaiah 40:31

If you are driving on a long trip, you may know that it is never a waste of time to stop for fuel. It is not cool to be walking down the road with a gas can in your hand because you ran out of gas. We have a destination we need to get to, but we must stay charged up. David learned the advantage of waiting on the Lord, getting his candle lit and his spirit charged up. Psalm 18:28 tells how David's candle was "lit up" so that he could run through the troop, leap over walls, pursue enemies, overtake them and trample them under his feet.

The power that charges you up is resurrection power coming from the indwelling presence of the Holy Spirit. God is able to do for us according to the measure of the power that is working in us. God has all the power we need, but we are not able to receive and release it in our lives unless we stay continually plugged in and charged up.

One of my heroes of faith, Smith Wigglesworth, wrote a book called *Ever Increasing Faith*. Here are some of my favorite quotes on the Holy Spirit from that book:

- *I see everything as a failure except that which is done in the Spirit.*
- *You can do more in one year if you are filled with the Holy Spirit than*

you can do in fifty years apart from Him.

- *It's impossible to over-estimate the importance of being filled with the Holy Spirit.*
- *There is nothing impossible to a man that is filled with the Holy Spirit.*
- *When you are filled with the Spirit, then you will know the voice of God.*
- *The moment you are filled with the Holy Spirit persecution starts.*
- *Anyone who is filled with the Holy Spirit might at any moment have any of the nine gifts of the Spirit in manifestation.*
- *Being filled with the Holy Spirit is not a luxury, it is a divine commandment.*

Joy is the bridge between believing and receiving.

(1 Peter 1:8-9)

8

THE NORTH SIDE OF THE MOUNTAIN

...for I know whom I have believed, and am persuaded that he is able to keep that which I have committed unto him against that day.
2 Timothy 1:12

Several years ago I bought Trina a beautiful baby grand piano. I enjoy hearing her play and sing many of the old hymns we sang in church growing up. We have a piano tuner come to our house and tune the piano regularly. One day when I came home I heard beautiful classical music coming from our den. As I entered the room I began to talk to the gentleman as he tuned the piano. He said that our piano has a particularly "sweet" sound. I asked him what he meant by that and he said that some pianos just have a sweeter sound than others. He also said that piano manufacturers prefer to use the wood from spruce trees that grow in the highest parts of the mountains. The higher altitudes and the cold north winds make it difficult for trees to grow and survive. As a result, the wood grain usually grows stronger and finer together. He said most piano manufacturers actually prefer the wood that comes from the trees on the north side of the mountain. The finest piano manufacturers will only use the wood from the north side of these trees. This wood produces the sweetest sounds. I found it interesting that the sweetest music comes from the trees that have the most difficult environment.

THE SWEETEST SOUND ON EARTH

Many times we face difficult situations in life that threaten to destroy us. However, if we will believe God and feed on His Word, He will strengthen us in every situation. ***The Holy Spirit will strengthen our inner man with mighty power and will enable us to stand.*** He will cause the "wood grain" to grow finer so that the "sweet sound" of grace and faith come from within. What the devil meant for destruction can actually cause you to turn to God with such faith that His grace is imparted unto your spirit and soul. What the devil meant for evil, God has turned for good!

The Apostle Paul went through great adversity and yet played the "sweetest music" in Ephesians and his other letters. Many of the greatest men and women of God have faced all the challenges that come from the "north side" of the mountain. Yet refusing to quit, they have acted on the Word of God and found strength to do the will of God.

Today, we play a part in determining the sound that comes from our lives. What will we do when we are facing the pressures of life? What is the secret of surviving and finishing your course? The answer is in the Word of God.

> *My brethren, count it all joy when you fall into divers temptations; knowing this, that the trying of your faith worketh patience. But let patience have her perfect work, that you may be perfect and entire, wanting nothing.*
> *James 1:2-4*

GOD'S PERFECT AND ENTIRE PLAN

When you are facing different kinds of adversity, don't lose your joy. The joy of the Lord is our strength (Nehemiah 8:10). The joy of the Lord will strengthen your inner man and fortify your faith.

In Philippians 4:4 Paul said, *"Rejoice in the Lord always...."* How can you rejoice in the middle of trouble? Because you KNOW that the trying of your faith works patience and brings you into God's perfect and entire plan (James 1:2-4). You must KNOW something other people don't. Paul said, *"I KNOW whom I have believed,"* 2 Timothy 1:12. In Job 19:25, Job said, *"I KNOW that my Redeemer liveth."* Job declared his faith in the midst of adversity (Job 5:22).

Many miss the importance of the joy aspect of faith. 1 Peter 1:8-9 says, *"Yet believing, you rejoice with joy unspeakable and full of glory, receiving the end of your faith."* Once you know and understand this, you will no longer get angry or depressed in times of adversity. Instead you will act on the Word of God. The wood grain will grow strong and fine in your spirit and you will overcome. Get ready for the sweet sound of victory that gives glory to God!

*The Holy Spirit takes
the things that belong to
the Father and Jesus and
transmits them to you.*

9

MAKE ROOM FOR THE HOLY SPIRIT

Even the Spirit of truth; whom the world cannot receive, because it seeth him not, neither knoweth him: but ye know him; for he dwelleth with you, and shall be IN you.

John 14:17

When Jesus spoke of the Holy Spirit, He said that He is not just coming to visit, but He is going to move and dwell in you permanently. That means the Holy Spirit is moving in. He is going to have a change of address. If you are going to visit someone, you only bring some of your stuff. But if you are moving in, you bring **ALL** of your stuff.

ALL things that the Father hath are mine: therefore said I, that he shall take of mine, and shall show it unto you.

John 16:15

EVERYTHING that the Father has is Mine. That is what I meant when I said that He [the Spirit] will take the things that are Mine and will reveal (declare, disclose, transmit) it to you.

AMP

The Holy Spirit takes the things that belong to the Father and Jesus and transmits them to you. If you are filled with the Holy Spirit, then you are filled with God. The Holy Spirit will expand you to make room for all He has for you.

When the Holy Spirit moves in, He is glad to be there. However, He needs room to bring all of His stuff. He can't get His stuff in until you get some of your stuff out. We are commanded to be filled with the Spirit.

And be not drunk with wine, wherein is excess; but be filled with the Spirit.

Ephesians 5:18

COOKED IN THE BATTER

One of my favorite things to eat is blueberry pancakes. Trina doesn't fix them for me at the house because she knows I have enough trouble already with my weight. She gives me wheat toast instead.

If I go out to eat somewhere that serves blueberry pancakes I always ask the server, "Do these blueberry pancakes just have blueberries poured on them or are the blueberries cooked in them?" Once you have had blueberry pancakes with the blueberries cooked in them, you don't want to eat them any other way. When I eat blueberry pancakes I want the blueberries cooked in the batter. Every bite I take, I want to hit a blueberry.

In the Old Testament, they just had blueberries (the Holy Spirit) on them. In the New Testament, the blueberries were cooked right in the batter. In other words, when you are filled with the Holy Spirit, nothing in life can take a bite out of you without hitting a blueberry. When the devil takes a bite out of you, you can say, "Ha, ha, ha, devil, you just hit a blueberry! You just hit the Holy Ghost living on the inside of me!"

The way you yield to the Holy Spirit is the same way you yield to all the will of God for your life.

10

YIELD TO THE HOLY SPIRIT

I heard the story of a man who was in a service where the Holy Spirit was moving. The Spirit of God began to move and the Holy Spirit manifested in great joy and freedom. The minister walked up to the man and asked, "Why don't you yield to the Holy Spirit?"

The man thought, "Yield, that's an interesting concept." He pulled out his Greek lexicon from his coat pocket to look up the word. In Greek, *yield* means "when a soldier presents himself to his commanding officer for orders." This word *yield* shows us how important it is for each of us to acknowledge the Holy Spirit every day. We must recognize, respect, receive and respond to the Holy Spirit.

RECOGNIZE THE HOLY SPIRIT

Don't suppress the Spirit...
1 Thessalonians 5:19 (MSG)

Is it possible to suppress or resist the Holy Spirit? In Acts 7:51, Stephen spoke these words to the leaders of the synagogue, "...ye do always resist the Holy Spirit." If we are not sensitive to the Holy Spirit, we can override anything He wants to say. Ephesians 4:30 says, "And grieve not the Holy Spirit of God...." God will not violate our right to choose. We must learn to recognize the Holy Spirit and welcome Him into our lives daily.

RESPECT THE HOLY SPIRIT

The Holy Spirit is the Greater One who lives on the inside of us. Jesus said of the Holy Spirit in John 14:17, "...the Spirit of Truth...ye know him; for he dwelleth with you, and shall be in you." We need to reverence and respect the Holy Spirit in us and report to Him for orders.

RECEIVE THE HOLY SPIRIT

The Holy Spirit can do more in five minutes than you can do in five years.

Smith Wigglesworth

There are so many things in this life that want to demand and command our time. Feelings are the voice of your body. Reason is the voice of your mind or soul. Your conscience is the voice of your spirit. The Holy Spirit will not force His way into your life. The Holy Spirit is a gentleman. He will only go where He is invited.

We must receive and make room for the Holy Spirit in our lives. Smith Wigglesworth also said:

No full gospel, Holy Ghost person should ever get out of bed in the morning without being filled with the Holy Spirit, getting lost in the Holy Spirit, and praying in the Holy Ghost.

RESPOND TO THE HOLY SPIRIT

Romans 8:14 says, "For as many as are led by the Spirit of God, they are the sons of God." The Holy Spirit is not going to make us do anything. He just prompts us. It is then our decision to respond to Him. If we would listen and respond to the Holy Spirit, we could avoid trouble in every area of our lives because He knows everything. We must yield and not resist the Holy Spirit.

THE ANOINTING ABIDES IN YOU

But the anointing which ye have received of him abideth in you....
                                        1 John 2:27

The Spirit of God lives in us. He is there to help us in every area of our lives. We must learn to recognize, respect, receive, and respond to the Holy Spirit. Instead of resisting the Holy Spirit, we must learn to yield to the anointing on the inside of us. The Holy Spirit will lead, instruct, and teach us as we recognize, respect, receive, and respond to Him.

The outpouring of the
Holy Spirit and times
of refreshing from the
presence of God.
(Acts 3:19)

11

OUTPOURINGS OF THE SPIRIT OF GOD

In 1906, one of the greatest outpourings of the Holy Spirit occurred in California at Azusa Street. From this outpouring, revivals were sparked all over the world. In the article <u>History of the Azusa Street Revival</u> from the "Azusa Street Centennial," you will see a brief summary of the history and impact of the Azusa Street revival:

> *While great revivals were taking place around the world at the turn of the 20th century, perhaps the most noted outpouring prior to the Los Angeles revival occurred in January 1901 at the Bethel Bible School in Topeka, Kansas taught by Charles*

Parham. After studying the Bible and spending time in prayer, several students experienced the Baptism of the Holy Ghost and began to speak in other tongues. Agnes Ozman is reported to have been the first to receive the experience, followed by several other students and the teacher, Charles Fox Parham. Meanwhile, William Seymour was traveling throughout the United States in search of a better life. An African-American from Louisiana, he was the son of former slaves. In 1905 Seymour traveled to Houston, Texas, in search of relatives. There he attended a black holiness congregation pastored by Lucy Farrow. Farrow moved to Kansas City to serve as a governess and cook for evangelist Charles Fox Parham, at which time Seymour became the interim pastor for the holiness congregation in Houston. In the late fall of 1905, Farrow returned to Houston and testified of her spiritual experience. She had been baptized with the Holy Ghost with the evidence of speaking in other tongues. Soon after Farrow returned to Houston, Parham relocated his ministry there as well.

Parham conducted services in Bryan Hall and taught training classes on many subjects including the Holy Spirit. Seymour was faithful in attending

Parham's services and training sessions. However, due to segregation laws of the time Seymour was forced to sit in the hallway while listening to Parham and others teach. Nonetheless, Seymour hungered for more of God and was determined to learn.

In 1905, Los Angeles resident Neely Terry, who attended a small holiness church pastored by Julia Hutchins, made a trip to Houston, Texas. She attended the church that William Seymour was pastoring. Impressed by Seymour's character and messages on the Holy Spirit he received an invitation to minister at the church in Los Angeles.

Seymour arrived in Los Angeles on February 22, 1906 and began preaching two days later. On April 9, 1906, a breakthrough occurred as Edward Lee was baptized with the Holy Spirit and began to speak in tongues after Seymour had prayed with him. The two men made their way to the Asbury home. There they had a song, prayers and testimonies, followed by Seymour's sermon using Acts 2:4 as a text.

The crowds became too large for the Asbury home on Bonnie Brae Street and were moved to the yard. Soon this became too limited as well. The group then discovered an available building at 312 Azusa Street, which had originally been constructed as an

*African Methodist Episcopal Church. Thousands
learned of the revival and were drawn to the meeting
from all over the world.*

*On the platform, a black man [Seymour] sat behind
two wooden boxes, one on top of the other. They
were his pulpit....Occasionally, as Pastor Seymour
prayed, his head would be so low that it disappeared
behind the top wooden box.... Many times waves of
glory would come over the meeting room, and people
would cry out prayers of thanks or praise as they
received the baptism of the Holy Spirit.*

*This move of God was not only for Los Angeles, but
it was for the whole world – even future generations.
Ultimately hundreds of millions have been reached
as an indirect result of Azusa Street.*

We are living in the last days before the return of
Christ. This generation needs the same outpouring
and times of refreshing of the Holy Spirit they had in
the book of Acts (Acts 3:19). In the book of Joel, God
said in the last days, He would pour out His spirit on
all flesh (Joel 2:28). In the book of Acts, Peter said:

**Ye men of Judaea, and all ye that dwell
at Jerusalem, be this known unto you,**

and hearken to my words: For these are not drunken, as ye suppose, seeing it is but the third hour of the day. But this is that which was spoken by the prophet Joel; And it shall come to pass in the last days, saith God, I will pour out of my Spirit upon all flesh: and your sons and your daughters shall prophesy, and your young men shall see visions, and your old men shall dream dreams: And on my servants and on my handmaidens I will pour out in those days of my Spirit; and they shall prophesy.

Acts 2:14-18

This Jesus God raised up, and of that all we [His disciples] are witnesses. Being therefore lifted high by and to the right hand of God, and having received from the Father the promised [blessing which is the] Holy Spirit, He has made this outpouring which you yourselves both see and hear.

Acts 2:32-33 (AMP)

Then Peter said unto them, Repent, and be baptized every one of you in the name of Jesus Christ for the remission of sins, and ye shall receive the gift of the Holy Ghost. For the promise is unto you, and to your children, and to all that are afar off, even as many as the LORD our God shall call.

Acts 2:38-39

I love what Dad Hagin said, *"The world needs to be taught to receive Jesus, but the church needs to be taught to receive the Holy Spirit."* Today, there are more than 600 million Spirit-filled, charismatic, Pentecostal believers that are changing nations. It is time for us to experience the glory of God in our generation.

ACKNOWLEDGMENTS

Special thanks to my wife, Trina.

My son, Aaron and his wife, Errin Cody; their daughters, Avery Jane and Macy Claire, their son, Jude Aaron.

My daughter, Alicia and her husband, Caleb; their sons, Jaiden Mark, Gavin Luke, Landon James, and Dylan Paul, their daughter Hadley Marie.

My parents, Pastor B.B. and Velma Hankins, who are now in Heaven with the Lord.

My wife's parents, Rev. William and Ginger Behrman.

ABOUT THE AUTHORS

Mark and Trina Hankins travel nationally and internationally preaching the Word of God with the power of the Holy Spirit. Their message centers on the spirit of faith, who the believer is in Christ, and the work of the Holy Spirit.

After over forty years of pastoral and traveling ministry, Mark and Trina are now ministering full-time in campmeetings, leadership conferences, and church services around the world and across the United States. Their son, Aaron, and his wife Errin Cody, are now the pastors of Christian Worship Center in Alexandria, Louisiana. Their daughter, Alicia Moran, and her husband Caleb, live in Lafayette, Louisiana. Mark and Trina have eight grandchildren.

Mark and Trina have written several books. For more information on Mark Hankins Ministries, log on to our website, www.markhankins.org.

Mark Hankins Ministries Publications

SPIRIT-FILLED SCRIPTURE STUDY GUIDE

A comprehensive study of scriptures in over 120 different translations on topics such as: Redemption, Faith, Finances, Prayer and many more.

THE BLOODLINE OF A CHAMPION

The blood of Jesus is the liquid language of love that flows from the heart of God and gives us hope in all circumstances. In this book, you will clearly see what the blood has done FOR US but also what the blood has done IN US as believers.

TAKING YOUR PLACE IN CHRIST

Many Christians talk about what they are trying to be and what they are going to be. This book is about who you are NOW as believers in Christ.

PAUL'S SYSTEM OF TRUTH

Paul's System of Truth reveals man's redemption in Christ, the reality of what happened from the cross to the throne and how to apply these realities for victory in life through Jesus Christ.

THE SECRET POWER OF JOY

If you only knew what happens in the Spirit when you rejoice, you would rejoice everyday. Joy is one of the great secrets of faith. This book will show you the importance of the joy of the Lord in a believer's life.

11:23 – THE LANGUAGE OF FAITH

Never under-estimate the power of one voice. Over 100 inspirational, mountain-moving quotes to "stir up" the spirit of faith in you.

LET THE GOOD TIMES ROLL

This book focuses on the five key factors to heaven on earth: The Holy Spirit, Glory, Faith, Joy, and Redemption. The Holy Spirit is a genius. If you will listen to Him, He will make you look smart.

THE POWER OF IDENTIFICATION WITH CHRIST

Learn how God identified us with Christ in His death, burial, resurrection, and seating in Heaven. The same identical life, victory, joy, and blessings that are In Christ are now in you. This is the glory and the mystery of Christianity – the power of the believer's identification with Christ.

REVOLUTIONARY REVELATION

This book provides excellent insight on how the spirit of wisdom and revelation is mandatory for believers to access their call, inheritance, and authority in Christ.

FAITH OPENS THE DOOR TO THE SUPERNATURAL

In this book you will learn how believing and speaking open the door to the supernatural.

NEVER RUN AT YOUR GIANT WITH YOUR MOUTH SHUT

We all face many giants in life that must be conquered before we can receive and do all that God has for us. Winning the War of words is necessary to win the fight of faith. So...Lift your voice!

THE SPIRIT OF FAITH

If you only knew what was on the other side of your mountain, you would move it! Having a spirit of faith is necessary to do the will of God and fulfill your destiny.

GOD'S HEALING WORD by Trina Hankins

Trina's testimony and a practical guide to receiving healing through meditating on the Word of God.

This guide includes: testimonies, practical teaching, Scriptures & confessions, and a CD with Scriptures & confessions (read by Mark Hankins).

Mark Hankins Ministries

PO BOX 12863

ALEXANDRIA, LA 71315

318.767.2001

E-mail: contact@markhankins.org

Visit us on the web: www.markhankins.org

Resources

Amplified Bible. Zondervan Publishing House, Grand Rapids, MI 1972.

Barclay, William. *New Testament Words.* The Westminster Press, Philadelphia, PA, 1964.

Brain, Marshall. *How Stuff Works.* Charwell Books, Inc, Edison, New Jersey, 2001.

Carter, Howard. *Questions and Answers on Spirtual Gifts.* Harrison House, Tulsa, Oklahoma, 1976.

Cornish, Gerald Warre. *Saint Paul from the Trenches.* Spirit to Spirit Publications, Tulsa, Oklahoma, 1981.

Johnson, Ben Campbell. *The Heart of Paul, A Rational Paraphrase of the New Testament.* Word Books, Waco, Texas, 1976.

Jordan, Clarence. *The Cotton Patch Version of Paul's Epistles.* Assosicated Press, New York, New York, 1968.

Kawano, Kenji. *Warriors: Navajo Code Talker.* Northland Publishing Company, Flagstaff, Arizonia, 1990.

Laubach, Frank C. *The Inspired Letters in Clearest English.* Thomas Nelson and Sons, New York, New York, 1956.

Montgomery, Helen Barrett. *Centenary Translation of the New Testament.* The American Baptist Publication Society, Philadelphia, Pennsylvania, 1924.

Morgan, Louis. *"Azuza Street Centential," History of the Azuza Street Revival,* http://www.azusastreet100.net/history (accessed May 10, 2006)

Nelson, P.C. *Bible Doctrines.* Gospel Publishing House, Springfield, Missouri, 1971.

New English Version of the Holy Bible. Zondervan Bible Publishers, Grand Rapids, MI 1979.

Peterson, Eugene. *The Message, The Bible in Contemporary Language.* NavPress Publishing Group, Colorado Springs, CO, 2003.

Stalker, James. *The Life of St. Paul.* Zondervan Corporation. Grand Rapids, MI, 1983.

The Jerusalem Bible. Double Day and Company, Inc. New York, NY, 1968.

Translator's New Testament. The Brittish and Foreign Bible Society, London, England, 1977.

Wade, G.W. *The Documents of the New Testament.* Thomas Burby and Company, London, England, 1934.

Wigglesworth, Smith. *Ever Increasing Faith.* Gospel Publishing House, Springfield, MO, 1971.

Wuest, Kenneth S. *The New Testament, An Expanded Translation.* William B. Erdmans Publishing Company, Grand Rapids, Michigan, 1981.

NOTES: